£9·00

Frome

in old picture postcards volume 2

by
Michael McGarvie

European Library – Zaltbommel/Netherlands

I should like to express my gratitude to allt those who have generously lent me postcards for both volumes. There are too many to list individually but special mention must be made of A.J. Brimson, F. Chant, C.D. Coles, R.D. Goodall, Mrs. C. Hirons, A. Mullins, Mrs. Peakall, Miss E. Star, G. Quartley, and H.T. Vranch. They have outstanding collections which they kindly let me ransack in order to compile these books. I thank them warmly.

.

Second edition: 1992

GB   ISBN 90 288 2836 2 / CIP

© 1984 European Library – Zaltbommel/Netherlands

INTRODUCTION

When compiling the first part of *Frome in old picture postcards* I was lent many more postcards than I could use, thanks to the generosity of numerous well-wishers. Making a selection was a difficult but pleasant task and I had reluctantly to leave out many interesting postcards owing to the limitations of space. The volume was well received and soon went into a second edition. This has encouraged me and my publishers to offer to the public the second part of *Frome in old picture postcards*.

Such books are not simply exercises in nostalgia. The postcards which they contain are fascinating in their own right registering as they do the slowly changing face of the town. Local residents can sometimes pick out relatives or the houses where they lived in youth. In a word, old postcards give visual effect to the town's memory.

Books of old postcards, however, are not merely self-indulgent. Although the first priority is that the reader should enjoy such a book, it serves an important secondary purpose of making a permanent record of postcards which are historical documents of great significance in a local context. And a nation is but the sum of its many communities. Most old postcards are in the hands of private collectors. Their future ownership and whereabouts must be uncertain. The European Library's series 'in old picture postcards' has provided a catalyst to bring the best of them together so that if we lose sight of the originals at least we shall have an authentic copy.

Looking at a further selection of views of old Frome, one cannot escape the impression that in the past the town was a neater and prettier place than it is today when it has lost so many of its trees and gardens some of which were in the heart of the town. Frome was also a much dirtier place, although judging by the amount of litter still dropped in its streets, this aspect of the past has not completely vanished. The appearance of the town today owes much not only to its rise but also to its decline. Frome expanded in a dramatic way at the end of the seventeenth century so that about 1720 Daniel Defoe found it 'prodigiously increased', its trade 'wholly clothing' and forsaw its future as 'likely to become one of the greatest and wealthiest inland towns in England'. The failure of the wool trade ('rather declining than increasing' in 1791) led to a period of poverty and distress in the nineteenth century so that Thomas Clark, a Bridgwater businessman, who visited Frome frequently in the 1830's felt that the town was 'destined in due course to sink'. New or expanded industries — brass and iron founding, brewing and printing — improved matters but there was never enough money for wholesale rebuilding so the structure of the town remained physically entire down to our own day, albeit largely devoted to manufactures other than wool.

Although some people were lamenting the destruction of so many old buildings as early as 1927, by and large Frome survived as a complete and little altered example of a late seventeenth-early eighteenth century industrial town almost into the age of conservation. Its streets of artisans' dwellings, harmoniously built of local stone and gracefully blending into numerous hillsides, its sumptuous chapels, elegant mansions, gloomy factories and high Victorian houses, its rich embellishment of carving, wrought-iron and multifarious signs, combined threefold to create a whole of compelling, interest, distinction and charm.

The late 1950's and early 1960's were periods of blight in Britain when the speculator and the developer had his way with our architectural heritage practically unchecked. Even Bath could not be saved so it is hardly surprising that it was at this period that much of old Frome fell a victim to the bulldozer and the pickaxe. The laudable intention, not seriously challenged at the time, was to do away with ancient slums and replace them with decent modern housing. Other buildings were taken down to make way for new car parks or roads, or to save money on upkeep. The demolition of Keyford Home in 1956 opened the flood-gates to an orgy of destruction. Much of the Trinity area including The Mint, a particularly sad loss in retrospect, Bridge Street, Waterloo, one side of Broadway, and Union Street were levelled. The Swan Inn, High Place, Merchants Barton and the old National School disappeared. Even Grade I buildings such as the Blue House and Rook Lane Chapel were threatened. Fortunately the Blue House was saved, but Rook Lane Chapel still remains a problem being currently for sale at £46,000.

In the 1970's the climate of opinion changed both in local government circles and amongst the public at large. Wholesale demolition and redevelopment became frowned upon; the restoration of old properties became acceptable, even praiseworthy. What remained of the Trinity area was saved by the skin of its teeth and an imaginative restoration scheme by Mendip District Council is now nearing completion. The Secretary of State for the Environment himself stepped in to preserve late seventeenth century houses in Vallis Way and in 1976 a large part of Frome was declared to be a Conservation Area of National Importance.

The growing interest in industrial history and in the lives and work of the poor helped Frome which had the luck to have a history which by no stretch of the imagination could be considered aristocratic or elitist. For a time Frome was lionised by scholars of that ilk. Since, the town has steadily improved in appearance, many minor buildings having been well restored by their owners. Sheppards Barton, Catherine Hill House and the Railway Station are cases in point. There is still some erosion of good Victorian buildings, a phenomenon which needs watching.

In part 1 a postcard of the declaration of poll at the old Police Station after the General Election of 1906 is included. In this volume I have included a picture of the celebrations which followed the election of Lord Weymouth as M.P. in 1895. Frome's name again became part of the title of a Parliamentary constituency in 1983 when it was transferred from Wells to 'Somerton and Frome'. The name should, of course, be 'Frome and Somerton'. Frome was a Parliamentary borough from 1832 until 1885 and for long after the votes were counted and the declarations made here; it is a large town by Somerset standards with an authentic Parliamentary tradition and it is obvious to any fair-minded person that it should have the primacy. The present name does not even make alphabetical sense.

Frome cannot be divorced from its rural hinterland. In the past the town was largely controlled from outside its boundaries by the Earls of Cork and Orrery who lived at Marston House and were Lords of the Hundred and main Manor of Frome, and by the Marquesses of Bath at Longleat whose Manor of West Woodlands came into the heart of the town. The Champneys family of Orchardleigh and the Lords Stourton also had manors here. From Saxon times Frome was the centre of a Hundred, an administrative area whose chief organ of authority was a court which met at Modbury, a barrow on Buckland Down.

Vestiges of the power of the Hundred survived almost to 1894 when many of the villages it contained were grouped together in the Frome Rural District whose Council was a rather more effective and intimate instrument of government. It met in Frome and was only merged in the new District of Mendip in 1974. For centuries Frome was the centre of the local wool trade and to the town the clothiers of all the surrounding villages brought their goods for carriage to London. The town was, and is, their shopping and market centre. So to round off the portrait of Frome I have included some postcards of the villages not forgetting Corsley and Maiden Bradley which, although in Wiltshire, have always had a close connection with Frome.

General View of Frome.

No. 2426.

1. An unusual view over Frome looking north-west. It was taken from the chimney of the Electricity Works. On the left is Zion Chapel with the varied roofs of Catherine Hill below. In the centre is Singer's works fronting Bull's Meadow, an open space in the heart of the town, now covered by Westway and the car park. To the right of Singers is Waterloo, now vanished under the factory, and Henley Villas, demolished in 1983. The old market hall is on the extreme right. From a postcard dated 1906.

2. Frome Market Place in 1909. It was evidently a hot day and no one seems in much of a hurry. Changes include the demolition of Charles Waters' shop (left), one of several he owned in the town, taken down for road widening in 1938. The site is now occupied by Holfords. The big block on the right was a draper's shop run by Mrs. W.F. Carpenter. It was replaced by the Midland Bank after the First World War. The two gossiping women in the foreground seem posed, but not so the old man peering through the gap behind them. The children wear voluminous smocks.

MARKET PLACE ON MARKET DAY, FROME.

3. The Market Place in the early 1920's: the character of the market has not changed, but the dress of the customers has and motor buses have replaced the horses and carts evident in 1909. The weather, too, has changed for the worse. On the right, sandwiched between two high blocks of buildings, the new Midland Bank can be glimpsed. The bicycle in the foreground advertises Hayward & Taylor, a local butcher's.

The Floods, King St

ASashby, Frome

4. Until 1968 floods were a regular feature of Frome life. This postcard of about 1920, taken from a photograph by A.S. Ashby, whose advertisement can still be seen on his former premises on the corner of the Market Place and Bath Street, shows just how far the waters advanced up the Market Place and into King Street. The Angel Inn is recorded in 1665. Opposite are the offices of Harding & Sons, old-established auctioneers, now Quartleys, and Carpenter's shop (extreme right) where the Midland Bank now stands.

5. Floral display by Mr. Alfred Vincent (the distinguished, flower bedecked gentleman on the right), fishmonger and poulterer, adjoining his shop at 15 Cheap Street (now The Settle Bakery) in May, 1906. It was part of a fund raising campaign by the local Friendly Societies Council in aid of the Victoria Hospital which raised £19. 10s. in a week. The boy is Walter Minty, later a fish and chip retailer at 10 Catherine Hill.

6. Alfred Vincent (who was not camera shy) poses outside his shop in Cheap Street about 1920. The mistletoe and poultery indicate that Christmas is near. Vincents was founded about 1840 and included amongst its patrons the Earl of Cork, Lord St. Maur, besides 'the magistrates, clergy and gentry of Frome'. The hearts of customers were said to 'warm towards the inanimate but appertising display of feathered and furred game dependent from the hooks about the shop'.

Ye olde Houses, Frome.

7. The top end of Gentle Street still gives a good impression of what Frome looked like in the seventeenth century, although the high classical block of Knoll House, built in 1839, is intrusive and mars the picture. It was erected by Dr. Bush, who lived in The Hermitage (centre) for his son. The Wagon and Horses was a public house from before 1568 until about 1960. The cottage on the left is on the site of the house of William Gentell, who gave his name to the street. In the foreground is a Blue School boy. This card was produced by E.C. Eames, a Stony Street stationer, about 1910.

8. Frome photographers were not often given to taking pictures in the snow, so this postcard of Bath Street about 1907 is a rarity. The absence of traffic reveals the spacious dignity of this thoroughfare cut under an Act of Parliament in 1810. The extensive wrought-iron railings, taken away during the Second World War, completed and furnished the street in a way which is now sadly lacking. On the left are Argyll Chambers and in the centre one of Cockeys' handsome gas lamp standards.

9. Another wintry scene: Christchurch Street West, probably taken after the same snowfall as the previous card. The old Police Station on the left was built in 1856 to the design of Charles Davis, the city architect of Bath, in the Gothic style. It is complemented by the large villas which, however, were not put up until the end of the nineteenth century. The centre house is constructed in white lias, an unusual stone in Frome.

WHITTOX L⁰ FROME
K⁰

10. Whittox Lane is not as well-known as Cheap Street or Gentle Street, but is still one of the most attractive streets in the town. It was even more attractive in 1906, the date of this postcard. It gets the name from the Whittock family, Quaker tanners in Whatcombe Bottom. On the right is Melrose House, one of Frome's most interesting early mansions. The house at the top of the vista, at the entrance to Milk Street, was demolished when the Trinity area was cleared in the early 1960's.

Vallis Way.   Frome.   E 16599

11. Vallis Way was a place to linger in 1905 with all the atmosphere of a village street. It may be so again when the A362 is re-routed. On the left, Blue School boys stand at the entrance to Baker Street. All the buildings on the right, including the historic Swan Inn, were taken down in the early 1960's. The house on the extreme right has Venetian windows — flat-headed side lights with a higher, round-headed central light — like Argyll House and West Lodge.

BUTTS HILL. FROME

12. The corner of Butts Hill and Keyford Street has changed almost beyond recognition since this postcard was published about 1905. The butcher's shop on the right survives, but the Fire Station now stands in place of the two cottages in the centre. It was here that the quarters of the Monmouth rebels were hung in 1685. On the left (with bay window) is the Unicorn Inn, recorded in 1781, but now demolished. A notice directs people to the Achilles Motor Works where Frome's own car was made.

The Butts,   Jan 3rd/0 5.   Frome.   E 16808

13. Until the seventeenth century all able bodied men were obliged by law to practise archery so that they would be useful to the Militia in case of invasion. In Frome, as in every other town, butts were maintained for this purpose and the name has lingered on. This postcard of 1905 is, by accident or design, addressed to a Miss Butt. On the right is the Red Lion Inn which closed in 1982. The houses on the left lost part of their gardens when the road was widened between the wars.

14. This postcard of 1908 purports to show Portway, but it is, of course, Wallbridge, a name deriving from the parapeted bridge which crossed the Frome here as early as 1250. The Wallbridge Hotel, built and run by Walter Hutchings, was the grandest of the four Temperance hotels which existed in Frome at the time. It is now part of the Tax Office while the Wallbridge Post Office (right) is a café.

15. Fromefield about 1907 looking towards the entrance to Fromefield House, from a photograph by John Bell, perhaps the best of the early Frome photographers. Despite Frome's reputation for dirt, Fromefield looks neat and elegant, the walls and gardens well-tended and cared for. The name derives ultimately from the mediaeval Field of Frome, but was localized to this area in the eighteenth century.

16. Although the main road out of Frome to the north, Bath Road in 1909 had the character of a country lane. Some horse droppings and a parked hand cart provide the only hints that it might be used by traffic. The fields which lay beside the road had just begun to be utilized for sites on which to build pleasant villas on the outskirts of the town for the more substantial Frome tradesmen. The wall on the left limits the grounds of Fromefield House. Another postcard by Bell.

17. Keyford in 1909. This shows the Beehive crossroads with High Place (left) demolished for road widening in the late 1960's. The decorations are in honour of the Prince and Princess of Wales (later George V and Queen Mary) who had been visiting Longleat and were returning through the town. The royal party did not stop and caused much disappointment by using closed cars despite the warm weather.

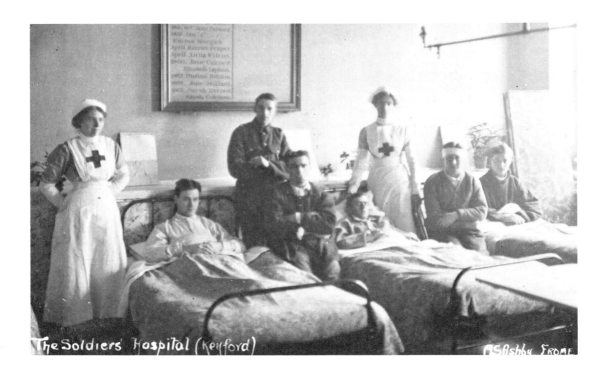

The Soldiers' Hospital (Keyford)

18. During the First World War Keyford 'Home' in Culverhill, which had been built as an asylum for girls and as a hospital for old men, became a real hospital for wounded soldiers. It was opened in November, 1914, and closed the following May having treated 588 in-patients and 13,980 out-patients. Here some of the less severely wounded men are seen with their nurses. Keyford 'Home' was demolished in 1956.

19. The firm of Samuel Rawlings & Son was one of the oldest in Frome. It claimed to have been founded in the mid-seventeenth century and only went out of business in the mid-1970's. Rawlings made cards for use in the woollen industry and leather straps for driving factory machinery. Their main factory was in South Parade and still stands. This is a rare glimpse of one of the firms' trade stands about 1911.

CATHERINE STREET, FROME

20. Catherine Street in the early 1920's showing the Sun Inn on the left. Opposite the inn are two well-known stores of the day, Coombs' Furniture and Dykes Fancy Bazaar. It was Coombs' boast that they sold furniture that was 'practically impossible to wear out', while Dyke's were noted not only for their postcards but also for china and glass including the now sort after 'crest of Frome' china.

21. Frome became a Parliamentary borough in 1832 and usually returned a Liberal M.P. In 1895, however, the Conservatives got in with Lord Weymouth who had a majority of 383 over his Liberal opponent, Sir John Barlow. Weymouth was the heir of Lord Bath whose extensive land and property holdings in the town may have helped him to turn the tide. Weymouth's tenure was short lived as the following year he succeeded his father as Marquess of Bath and went to the House of Lords. The two houses shown here have been demolished. They stood at the top of Bath Street opposite the Lamb Inn.

SIR JOHN & LADY BARLOW & FAMILY, COLWYN BAY, JULY 6 190

22. John Emmott Barlow (1857-1932), of Bradwell Hall in Cheshire, was M.P. for Frome from 1892 until 1895 and from 1896 until 1918. He was created a baronet in 1907. He is seen here on holiday at Colwyn Bay with his wife (the former Hon. Anna Denman, who died in 1965, aged 91) and four children: Nancy, Thomas, Anna Elizabeth (on her mother's lap) and John Denman Barlow, who succeeded his father as second baronet. He, too, became an M.P.

23. Church Steps and the Old Church House bedecked with flags to celebrate the end of
the First World War in 1918. Clowns and other members of the cast of an entertainment
held at the Palace Theatre to celebrate the victory of the Allies, pose in front of a car
decorated with patriotic fervour. The wreath strikes a more sombre note with its
inscription reading: 'In loving memory of our gallant dead.' A photograph by L.
Vearncombe, of Lock's Hill Studio, whose cards are rare.

24. The youth of 1912. Even before the First World War several institutions had their own sports clubs such as the Y.M.C.A. Association Football Club and the Holy Trinity Football Club. This postcard shows the Badcox Lane Football Club in 1911-12. It was founded by Henry G. Chislett (left), a builder, and associated with the chapel of the same name in Catherine Street (where Chislett had his premises) and played on a pitch at Welshmill, now occupied by Singer's car park.

25. Monster Sunday School processions on Whit-Monday, together with the distribution of buns, are a traditional feature of Frome church life. In this postcard of 1907 a procession, well bedecked with banners and flags, wends its way up Duke Street and debouches into Trinity Street. The picture gives a good impression of the gorge-like character of the streets in that part of the Trinity area which was cleared in the 1960's. On the right is one of Waters' chain of grocery shops.

26. The Blue House, which incorporates charities going back to the fifteenth century, was rebuilt in 1724 at a cost of £1,401 through the efforts of James Wickham, a local solicitor. This postcard of about 1910 is a good portrait of the handsome central block decorated with statues of an almswoman and a scholar of the foundation: 'Nancy Guy and Billy Ball up against the Blue — school wall.' Note the boys in their uniforms and the railings. The school closed in 1921.

27. Photographs of Blue School boys, who occupied the centre of the Blue House, are not uncommon. Much rarer are pictures of the 'Blue women' who were maintained under the original foundation of William Leversedge. There were fourteen of them receiving 5s. a week and living in the south wing (the north wing was given over to pauper women). Some of the 'Blue women' are seen here in their blue gowns of which they received one every two years.

28. N. Taylor's central motor and cycle depot was one of eight cycle agents and dealers in Frome in the 1920's when this postcard was made. His shop, since demolished, was in Catherine Hill next to what is now the Old Curiosity Shop. In 1925 he was advertising 'the Omega one point seven: two speed, kick start and clutch. The little bike with the big future' for £29. 10s. The photograph was taken by John Bell whose studios adjoined at Catherine Hill House.

29. In the early 1900's, Charles Waters had several grocer's shops round Frome with premises in Portway, Trinity Street (see no. 25), Fromefield and Catherine Street. His slogan was 'Don't live to eat, but eat to live'. This is another of his shops which stood at the corner of The Butts and Somerset Road. It has since been demolished. Outside stands the manager, Mr. Anstey. About 1910.

30. Smarter parts of the town required superior shops and Waters' grocery and provision
stores in Portway prided itself on the service provided. The shop is now the Wallbridge
Post Office. The delivery cart in the foreground enhances the interest of this well-
composed picture by an unknown photographer. On the right is the Coalash Walk with a
lamp standard and pillars by Cockey & Sons, the local ironfounders.

31. Charles Axford Bray began as a bill poster in the 1890's before establishing this printer's and stationer's business in Church Street. Later the firm was run by his daughter Ellen Bray (who died, aged 102, in 1983) and as the Ellenbray Press is still one of the leading names in the town, although now situated in Westway. The advertisement for postcards of the War Memorial at 3d. each suggests a date of about 1920.

32. Fund raising for good causes is still a familiar part of town life. This postcard of 1907 shows a concert organized by Frome Fire Brigade in aid of the Victoria Hospital and the Victoria Baths. Members of the Brigade stand at the back while in the centre is the venerable, white-bearded figure of W.B. Harvey, a noted townsman of the day. The venue is the old Market Hall.

33. The choir of St. John's Church in procession through the Market Place, probably during the patronal festival on 24th June. It is led by the churchwardens carrying their staves of office; censor, candles, cross and banner follow. In the background is the covered market which lay underneath the George Hotel Assembly Room, now all part of the National Westminster Bank. The placards advertise the sale of farms at Wanstrow and Batcombe and 'The Lady of Ostend', a farcical comedy, at the Palace. (1920's.)

34. Captain A.C. Duckworth (1870-1948), later Squire of Orchardleigh, was among the first of the local gentry to abandon the carriage and pair for a motor car. Here he is in his 12 h.p. 2 cylinder Argyll in 1904. Note the solid tyres and door at the back. The rain hood was an extra, added by Fullers of Bath, the first they made. It also acted as a dust screen — essential on the unmade-up roads of the time.

35. Lower Keyford was the centre of a tanning industry at least as early as 1666, but has left little in the way of records. The firm of Charles Case & Son was well-established by 1842 and transferred to Westbury about 1920. Its closure there this year has recently been announced. This postcard of the work force, whom it was always said could be identified from way off by the aroma which clung to them, is dated 1912.

36. With the Somerset Light Infantry, Cornwall and Somerset Royal Artillery and North Somerset Imperial Yeomanry based in Frome, military obsequies were not uncommon. Here a procession moves from Keyford towards Gorehedge, passing garden ground bounded by a neat wall now occupied by a builders' merchant. The occasion is probably the funeral of Sergeant-Major Spence, Drill Instructor at Keyford, who was buried at Christ Church with full military honours on 4th May, 1924. A postcard by A.E. Whittington, of Alexandra Road.

37. Frome was famous for its strong beer which the gentry were said to prefer to port or
French wine. Almost every public house had its own brewery. These were reduced to nine
in 1881, some of whom joined together to form the Frome United Breweries in 1889
with a big brewery between Broadway and Vallis Way which came down in 1959. The
rival concern, the Lamb Brewery, was demolished the same year. Here the beer is being
delivered about 1910.

38. The Wheatsheaves Inn is mentioned by name in 1731 and in 1822 was described as 'very good' and 'very elegantly fitted up'. Edward Mansford, a brandy merchant, tempted by the extensive cellars of the Wheatsheaves, set up as a wine and spirit dealer there in the 1820's. His son went into partnership with the Baily family, well-known brewers, and that Frome duality, Mansford & Baily was created. The name is still in general use. A postcard of 1909.

39. Tytherington was a hamlet in the old parish of Frome but is now in Selwood. William Davidge was retailing beer there in 1894. This is a rare view of one of the characteristic stone and thatched cottages of the area being demolished, presumably to make way for the present Fox and Hounds public house. There is no sign of fire. The notice reads: 'William Davidge. Licenced to sell beer, ale, porter & cider to drink on the premises.'

40. In 1907, Charles Houlton, of 2 Catherine Street, was one of forty-five grocers in Frome. His shop faced down Catherine Hill and was part of a block of property which jutted out into the roadway, narrowing it considerably. Such constructions were a feature of several streets in the town. In the background is the Temperance Hall. The shop was demolished in the 1920's.

CATHERINE STREET, FROME. (3)

94275.J.V.

41. Looking from the top of Catherine Hill into Catherine Street about 1925. On the left of the centre is Badcox Lane Chapel. Houlton's shop has gone. On the left is the Temperance Hall, built of local stone with Bath stone dressings in 1874. Both the architect, Joseph Chapman, and the builder, Thomas Parfitt, were teetotallers. The structure became unsafe and was taken down in 1964. Much of Frome's best photographic work came from Bell's Studio (centre).

Beckington.

Publ. by R. Wilkinson & Cº, Trowbridge.

42. Beckington, three miles north-east of Frome, was once a thriving wool town. It is said to have had five working factories as late as 1900 and is 'uncommonly rich in worthwhile stone houses' — the former homes of the wealthy clothiers. Beckington was also an educational centre with several private schools. This postcard of 1904 shows the main street, rather more peaceful than it is today.

43. Great Elm is about two and a half miles north-west of Frome. Settlement in the valley was encouraged by the presence of an edgetool manufactory deriving power from the waters of the Mells stream. This postcard of 1907 records much that has vanished: Elmhust (top right), a Gothic villa, burnt down in 1958, thatched houses near the bridge where Glenthorne now stands (left) and the rank of almshouses (right) now demolished. The arch (centre) survives, although the ruins behind have been cleared.

44. Since the picturesque first began to be appreciated in the eighteenth century, Elm has been noted for its beautiful and romantic scenery. Here Glenthorne, a typical Edwardian house, built by John Hampden Wall about 1908, has replaced the thatched cottages seen in the previous card. In place of the almshouses are Glenthorne's extensive glasshouses. The cottages ascend the hillside in a haphazard but natural way which is instinctively right.

45. Farleigh Hungerford, seven miles north of Frome, is famous for its castle. This postcard of about 1900 shows its industrial side. There was a fulling mill at Farleigh in 1548 and a factory on this site by the bridge in 1821. As Charles Salter & Co, woollen manufacturers, it survived until 1910 when the machinery was sold and the buildings demolished. No other picture of the mill is known.

46. From 1546 until 1949 the Longleat estate of the Marquess of Bath, owned a large part of the parish of Frome and many houses in the town. Longleat was also a great sporting estate, tempting to poachers from Frome which lay so close to the preserves. A small army of gamekeepers was employed by the Marquess to protect his coverts. Here sixteen of them, in the gaiters and corduroy trousers which seem 'de rigueur', face down the camera.

MOTORS AT LONGLEAT

47. Longleat was to some degree a show house long before it officially opened to the public in 1949. Crowds flocked there in 1789 to see George III and his family, while the interior was always shown when the Thynne family were away. By 1900 the house and grounds were already the venue for jamborees such as this hill climbing competition organized there by the Motor Union of Great Britain and Ireland on 21 July, 1906. Here the cars assemble in front of the house.

48. Lullington, three miles north of Frome, is mentioned in Domesday Book (1086) and has a church rich in Norman ornament. This postcard of 1910 shows the ancient cottages of the original village, stone built and thatched. The cottages on the right remain, but those on the left were burnt down and rebuilt by A.C. Duckworth, of Orchardleigh, in 1927.

Lullington.

Pub. by R. Wilkinson & Cº, Trowbridge

49. When the Duckworth family bought Lullington in 1855 there was only one cottage which did not belong to the estate. The village was so decayed that it was described as not worth having. William Duckworth created a model village, employing the architect George Devey to design new farms, cottages and a rectory. Mrs. Duckworth paid for the huge and ideosyncratic school (right) in 1858. (About 1910.)

50. Today heavy traffic thunders through Buckland Dinham, three miles north-west of Frome, making this rural scene, deserted except for two shire horses, difficult to credit. On the left is the Bell Inn. Buckland was not always so rustic having once had a weekly market and a yearly fair, granted by Henry III to Geoffrey de Dinham in 1239. The fair was held as late as 1875 on the eve, day and morrow of Michaelmas.

Buckland, Frome.

51. The cottages of Buckland Dinham lie scattered over the hillside by the road which ascends to St. Michael's Church. Apart from agriculture, the main occupation of Buckland in the past was the manufacture of cloth and the growing of teasels used in the trade. The double-barrelled name derives from the Dinham family who owned the village and 'book land' — land granted by charter (and so heritable) as opposed to free land.

52. On Sunday, 13th May 1906 there was a terrific thunderstorm over Frome and district accompanied by a cloud burst. Great damage was caused in the town as well as at Kilmersdon and Radstock. Riverside Cottage at Buckland Dinham was in the front line as water poured down the hillside and the level of the brook rose. The thatched roof of a haystack was carried one hundred yards to its owner's front door.

Storm havoc at
Coleford May 13 19

53. Coleford also suffered in the storm of May, 1906. In this postcard local people contemplate the damage. It gives a good view of 'Hucky Duck' the 'noble and stupendous aqueduct' built in 1801 to take the abortive Somerset and Dorset Canal across a tributary of the Emburough stream. The aqueduct, which originally had a parapet 4 to 6 feet high, was never used.

Havoc caused by a cloud burst MELLS May 18 1906

54. The great storm of May 1906 broke down walls all over the countryside. The grounds of Mells Rectory, three and a half miles west of Frome, were devastated. Such downpours were not unknown: at Mells in 1828 a storm turned roads into torrents in an hour, threw down walls in every direction and flooded every house 'more or less'. This postcard shows the village street with the Rectory Cottages and Tithe Barn in the distance.

Mells Village

Valentines Series

55. Mells was once a hive of industry, a seat of the cloth trade with so many fulling mills that they gave name to the village. From 1744 until 1894 edgetools were made here in great quantities. The original village clung to the rocky spine in the centre below the church tower. Thatch was the usual roofing material before clay tiles and slate came in. (About 1910.)

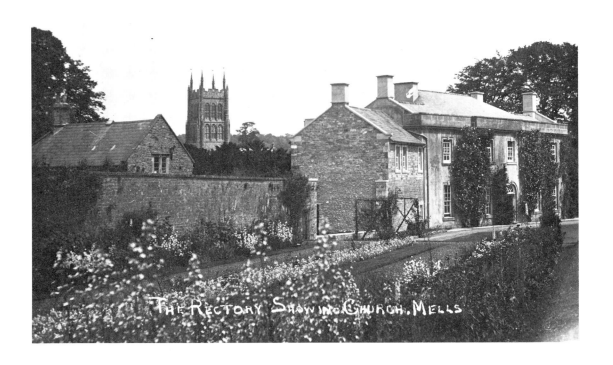

THE RECTORY SHOWING CHURCH. MELLS

56. Mells Rectory, a private house since 1982, was formerly the mansion of a family of clothiers named Jesser and the present house incorporates much of their building of about 1730. It became the rectory in 1762 when it was rebuilt and embellished by the Reverend Thomas Paget. The old rectory stood opposite New Street. This postcard of 1933 shows the house restored after a fire four years earlier.

Destruction of Mells Rectory by fire, Easter Monday, April 1st 1929.

57. The disastrous fire at Mells Rectory on Easter Monday, 1929, is still remembered in Mells. The building was gutted and although almost immediately restored, the third story which had dormer windows was not replaced. In the nineteenth century the rectory was 'set in a beautiful domain nearly a mile in extent of shubberies and plantations'; indeed, it was so grand that during the incumbency of Dr. Bishop the rectory was nick-named 'The Bishopric'.

58. Mells School about 1905. There was a grammar school at Mells in 1524, but the present school, one of the first five Church schools in Somerset, was not established until 1813 in what had been a weaving room on the left in this postcard. The school is still in use, although a new wing has been added on the right to what was once the head teacher's house. A separate boys' school was set up in 1840 in New Street.

Marston House

59. Marston House, two and a half miles south-west of Frome, was the seat of the Earls of Cork and Orrery from 1641 until 1905. Postmarked 1905, this card shows the main building whose recessed centre and extruded corners indicate its early seventeenth century origins, although 'modernized' in 1749-1752. The loggia is early nineteenth century while the wing (centre right) was added in 1776. After years of neglect, Marston is now in process of restoration.

60. The entrance front of Marston House from a postcard of 1907. The monumental doorway to the Grand Hall (on the left) with its massive pillars and pediment was built in 1858 to the design of Major Charles Davis, the Bath city architect. *Its exterior embellishments in stone carving... are imposing and elegant*, wrote a contemporary. On the right are the terraced gardens.

MAIDEN BRADLEY.

61. Maiden Bradley, six miles south of Frome, is in Wiltshire but as part of the Duke of Somerset's estate it always had close ties with Frome and its market. The name derives from a priory founded here in the twelfth century which was a refuge for leprous women. This view of the High Street, somnolent in the summer sun, was taken about 1906.

62. The funeral of Algernon St. Maur, fifteenth Duke of Somerset, at Maiden Bradley Church on 25th October, 1923. The Duke, noted for his height, strength and genial manner, had an adventurous life, including living among Canadian Indians, before succeeding to the dukedom in 1894 and settling 'among his own people in the ancient village which lies between the Wiltshire Downs and the spacious woods reaching away to the blue distances of Somerset'. He was buried on Brimble Hill Clump.

Nunney Castle and Village.

63. Nunney, three and a half miles south-west of Frome, is well-known for its unusual castle, built under royal licence by Sir John de la Mare in 1373. When this picture was taken about 1912, the castle was a neglected ruin, the ramparts festooned with plants, the moat filled with rubbish and a curtain wall collapsed. On the left is a corner of the Manor House and on the right the tower of All Saints' Church.

Nunney Castle.
This picturesque 14th century Castle bears
the marks of a siege which it sustained during
the Great Rebellion, when it was garrisoned in
the Royalist Cause by Sir John Dalyrmple, but
was taken by the Parliamentarians in 1645.

64. Picturesque and romantic in decay: Nunney Castle and brook in 1908. The owner
refused to repair the structure and it was not until 1929 that it was put into the care of
the old Ministry of Works and the ruins carefully conserved. The castle is symmetrical in
plan, but so narrow that the towers almost meet at the ends.

65. An unusual view of Nunney village about 1920, probably taken from the top of the church tower. In the centre is Cobblers Cottage with its distinctive high, narrow structure. Anciently Nunney depended for its prosperity on the wool trade and later had a flourishing manufactory of edgetools. Henry III granted the village a market and fair in 1260.

66. Orchardleigh House, two and a half miles north of Frome, was built by William Duckworth in 1856-1858 to the designs of T.H. Wyatt. It cost about £40,000 and was intended to be a combination of an Elizabethan country house and a French renaissance château, cheerful and comfortable rather than pretentious and ornamental. The Conservatory has lost its roof and glass since this picture was taken about 1908.

67. From 1440 until 1839 Orchardleigh belonged to the Champneys family, the last of whom, Sir Thomas S. Mostyn-Champneys, spent £100,000, perhaps £2,000,000 in modern money, improving the park. He created the lake, put a moat round the church, and built numerous lodges in various styles of architecture, often well decorated with heraldry for he was obsessively proud of his ancestors. This is the Gothic Nightingale Lodge, erected about 1810, as it was in 1909.

Falkland Tower.

68. Turner's Tower at Faulkland in Hemington, six miles north-west of Frome, 185 feet high, was one of the most curious Somerset follies. It was built by Thomas Turner, a local resident, to outrival the column put up at nearby Ammerdown in memory of T.S. Joliffe in 1857. This it did. The upper part was of wood. Below were a dance hall and tea gardens. The project was not a financial success and the tower was taken down in stages.

WANSTROW.

69. Wanstrow is on the road to Bruton, six miles south-west of Frome. The village, once well-known for its pottery, is grouped around a crossroads. This card, which bears the Wanstrow postmark for 22nd July 1905, is a view looking west over the crossroads towards St. Mary's Church. The William IV Inn is centre left. The sender asks: 'How do you like this P.C.? There are several different ones of the village.'

70. A later view of Wanstrow looking east towards the Primitive Methodist Chapel. The card is postmarked 1937. In the past much of Wanstrow belonged to Wells Cathedral and supported a prebend. The village is mainly occupied in dairy farming and was one of the first in the area to receive a piped water supply, this coming from the springs at Dursley.

71. Kilmington, six miles south of Frome, in 1906. This is that part of the scattered parish known as Kilmington Street and it is close to Blatchwell Spring, the source of the River Wylie. Kilmington belonged to Somerset until 1896, a curiosity, probably of manorial origin, as geographically it is part of Wiltshire and was surrounded on three sides by that county.

72. Witham Station was built in the early 1850's when the Wiltshire, Somerset and Weymouth Railway was extended from Frome. To those interested in railway architecture it was significant because designed in the office of I.K. Brunel — probably by R.P. Brereton — and characteristic of the great man's style. Witham Station was familiar to many as the junction for Shepton Mallet and Wells. It closed in the early 1960's and has since been completely destroyed.

WITHAM FRIARY

73. Six miles south-west of Frome Witham Friary is a remote village situated in the vale of the same name. The stone vaulted parish church, seen in the postcard of the 1920's, was the lay brothers' chapel of the Carthusian monastery founded here by Henry II about 1178. Postcards of Witham are rare although the writer of this card says 'there are two or three more'.

74. Whatley, three miles west of Frome, is now dominated by the quarry industry and this quiet lane has become a busy road. There is a fine church with a spire and notable old farmhouses. Whatley once enjoyed a fair granted by Henry VI in 1442. This postcard of about 1905 shows Whatley Lodge on the left with the turning to Nunney and on the right Little Combe, covered in creeper and looking the worse for wear.

Corsley.

75. Among the hamlets of Corsley is Middle Whitbourne, formerly called Temple from the Knights Templar who once owned it. There was an ancient chapel here, but the church seen in this postcard of about 1914 is St. Mary's built in 1902 with £4,300 left for the purpose by Mrs. Barton, of Corsley House. It seats 120 people. The cottage on the right has now disappeared.

Meet of the South & West Wilts Foxhounds, Alfred's Tower, Stourhead. (Copyright.)

76. Alfred's Tower, seen here in 1905, is on the Stourhead estate, but actually in the Somerset parish of South Brewham. The tower is a triangular structure of red brick 150 feet high and stands on Kingsettle Hill 800 feet above sea level. It was built by Henry Hoare in 1770-1772, designed by Henry Flitcroft, and commemorates Alfred the Great, 'the founder of the English Monarchy and Liberty'.